Moving Beyond

Moving Beyond

Toward Transformative *Theologizing*

KAREN L. BLOOMQUIST

WIPF & STOCK · Eugene, Oregon

MOVING BEYOND
Toward Transformative *Theologizing*

Wipf & Stock
An Imprint of Wipf and Stock Publishers
199 W. 8th Ave., Suite 3
Eugene, OR 97401

www.wipfandstock.com

PAPERBACK ISBN: 979-8-3852-1375-7
HARDCOVER ISBN: 979-8-3852-1376-4
EBOOK ISBN: 979-8-3852-1377-1

04/19/24

Contents

Contents

Introduction

THIS SHORT BOOK IS intended to reach those who are turned off by numerous footnotes. It is not intended as a scholarly work. Hundreds of books and authors has influenced me through the years, some of which are on the shelves in my home. Only a few are cited here. Most pieces were written since 2019.

This is not really a memoir, although it draws quite selectively from what I have experienced, and that have resulted in what may be at times provocative. My late husband Bill and son Aaron are not mentioned, although both have influenced me.

Because the theme is *theologizing*, it is intended to stir others to do this in the face of contextually-based challenges. Thus, the theme here is not fully fleshed out, but only suggestive of what needs to be done in relation to local settings and timely developments. These require not repetition of theological platitudes but ongoing theologizing in the face of such.

CHAPTER 1

Some pivotal perspectives

Transformative theologizing[1]

Theologizing is an ongoing, transforming process in the world. Theology may be dying when it becomes only rhetoric or allegiance to a given tradition, especially to gain funding, whether from local, national, or global sources.

IN THE 1970s, I decided to work on a PhD in theology, even though my interests were pulling me into ethics. Back then, Lutheran ethics was seen by many as an oxymoron: "God does it all; we don't." Because I wanted to be a *real* theologian, I began with theology, but what really tugged at me were the social/ethical issues of the time. The conjunction was key: my first teaching position was in "church and society," and in the Lutheran World Federation (LWF), besides directing the theological unit, my chair was "church and social issues." The assumption operating in both cases

1. An earlier version of this was in the October–November 2022 online *Journal of Lutheran Ethics:* www.elca.org/Faith/JLE.

1

was that the church and its theology were somehow fixed and separate from ever-changing society or social issues, and these need to be bought together. Theology is popularly seen only as other-worldly.

Inspired by various liberation theologies that were emerging in the 1970s, especially focused on those who have been marginalized (those who are black, feminist, etc.), and what I observed while growing up in and serving mainly working-class congregations, I decided to bring these insights together for my doctoral dissertation on theologically understanding and responding to white working-class realities. I realize now that this was the beginning of moving from static theology to dynamic *theologizing*. Rather than simply applying what have been theological formulations of the past, these need to be re-interpreted or applied in new ways if they are to be redemptive (or transformative) of what is holding working-class folks in bondage in a given historical context. *Class* has been an overlooked reality then and now, which may be why many are succumbing to right-wing appeals.

In the early 1980s, when I started teaching at the Lutheran School of Theology in Chicago, an article focused on me with the heading, "Prophet for the '80s fights racism."[2] My teaching was influenced by much that was occurring in liberation theologies. My theological method chart began with "what's going on with folks"(step 1), raising the systematic analysis question, "why it it like this?" (step 2), asking "what is Good News in relation to this reality?" (step 3), and finally "what needs to be done differently in light of this?" (step 4). As I was reminded by one of my mentors Dorothee Soelle, the fourth step—action/ *praxis*—reveals new realities or tensions that themselves

---

2. Larson, "Prophet for the 80s."

call for further theological reflection, especially as we interact with those who are different from ourselves. New challenges and tensions arise, which themselves provoke further theologizing. Step three is not the end; this leads into further and unending theologizing, theological reflection on what was occurring.

In my years with the Lutheran World Federation, I realized how few from the global South thought of themselves as *theologians*, choosing instead to pursue biblical studies or pastoral care. Theology may have been too intimidating, associated with what Europeans had refined over centuries. Theology was experienced as abstract or elitist, not in touch with what people were actually facing in daily life. I recall a Tanzanian theologian's real concern was focused on how a tiger might eat her aging father. In teaching an online course, when some US students complained about the economic realities they were facing, the head of an African seminary replied that he had not even been paid for many months. Funding for practical projects was and still is far more popular than *theological studies*. Theology can become only rhetoric or allegiance to a given tradition, especially to gain funding, whether from local, national or global sources. Of what concrete, earthly good is theology?

Increasingly today, studies in *diakonia* and theology are combined. For many, theology mostly impels the real action of practical action in the world, of *diakonia*. That is what matters, and indeed, it is. However, the ongoing need to theologize in light of what is occurring in practice is usually overlooked. Theology becomes the motivating force, a send-off or point of departure. This is important, but not sufficient. Theologizing that occurs in light of practice is what matters.

In highly secular societies, such as where I now live, people glaze over when you state you are a theologian. Theology is increasingly marginalized, considered quaint, of a bygone era. It often is associated with doctrine, and is rooted there, but too often it becomes static or is felt as doctrinaire or judging. Many people claim to be *spiritual,* which for them is other-worldly and free floating, not connected with religious institutions. These institutions have experienced significant declines in recent years. They often are associated popularly with right-wing, rather than with justice-seeking agendas and movements in the world. There is a considerable amount of skepticism regarding religion, especially given how much negative attention it is getting in the media. Many ask, can there be any earthly good associated with religion today?

Historical examples of what religion has done, or been used for, only reinforce the popular impression of religion. Many now reject religion as having any earthly good. Too often religion has been a dividing force throughout history. This includes the repeated colonization of those thought of as *other*, crusades against those of another religion, supremacy of Christians over others, and various expressions and practices of empire. Many have analyzed and decried such.

Recently some have raised up what Jesus did to cross boundaries rooted in culture, gender or racial constructs, or nationality or religion. Instead, religion is often misused and weaponized by the Christian Right (or by other dominant religions). Too often it is being used for nationalist political agendas.

I propose that rather than referring to theology as a fixed noun, *theologizing* is a verb. Its focus is ongoing processes of what God is doing. This is not only contextual but also actually transformative of what is. Theologizing has the power to change (transform) what is unjust and systemic in societies, with a much different worldview that what has become dominant. Enacting another worldview than what currently is reigning and dominating is what *theologizing* does. It does this not in a stand-apart, static way, but in ways that are collaborative and eventually transformative of what actually is occurring here and now. This is theologizing.

This means knowing theological traditions well through biblical, historical and other studies, finding what is key in them, but going beyond so as to draw from them in creative ways in ever new situations. It is not unchanging but ongoing. This changes with contexts and challenges, and is transformative of them toward more justice.

The biblical account of the Magnificat in Luke (1:46ff) has emphasized Mary's low estate and humbleness, and her praise of what God has done. However, in recent years, what has been emphasized are verses 52–54. God has brought down the powerful, and lifted up the lowly, or the revolutionary acts of resisting and turning over oppressive rule. This is exemplified in the hymn *Canticle of the Turning*,[3] which is an example of transformative theologizing. It involves looking again at traditional texts, which today speak with new urgency about the challenging contexts we face today, and have not been sufficiently emphasized in centuries of doctrinal imposition. Too often the text has been de-politicized to make it more acceptable to established order, and especially to keep women submissive. In the Magnificat the whole being of Mary is emphasized. The Word is not passive but enacts an alternative vision and power.

3. *Evangelical Lutheran Worship*, 723.

Whereas theology can be seen as a set of doctrines or a noun, the verb *theologizing* is an ongoing process of what is Good News here and how. This continues to change with and reflects on practice. This does not mean that all is up for grabs. There is a core that does not change with circumstances—a grammar bordered by grace, love of neighbor, the cross, and so forth, that must be deeply learned if it is to be applied in ever new situations—that are "recoded and rewired within new semantic fields."[4]

I wrote some years ago that the value of theology is in terms of the questions it raises, and the new spaces it opens up for confessing and living out the faith in current contexts. Renewal in theology, worship and church life does not simply mean going back to tradition, but it involves retrieving, revising, recasting and transfiguring what has been received. How to think and write theologically, rather than only repeating answers others provide, is a skill or art that urgently needs to be developed through more appropriate methodologies and pedagogies.[5] I now am referring to this as *theologizing*.

What is taught in theological schools and courses often is what was meant in biblical times and in doctrinal developments since then. This is important, but it must not stop there. Theology is ongoing. Through theological studies students are being prepared not just to repeat these formulae but to creatively envision, embody, and enact how this is transformative in ever new contexts and challenges today. It is assumed that when they leave theological studies much of what students have learned through these studies should be set aside. It is assumed that those in local

4. Bloomquist, ed. *Transformative Theological Perspectives*, 26.

5. Bloomquist, ed. *Transformative Theological Perspectives*, 193, 196, 204.

congregations just want to hear the familiar formulas, and are uneasy if a preacher or teacher challenges such or brings in new connections with challenges today, especially if this has political implications. Theology remains otherworldly.

Those with this creative spirit often leave congregations, and turn to other vocations or expressions that are more artistic and less pedantic for communicating what faith involves. These often express what theologizing is about. Many of the issues and challenges we face today were not obviously present in biblical times, or since then, but what is communicated through theologizing is new or different from what was expressed then. New meanings or connections are made. Yet these are rooted in the grammar of the faith as expressed through a theological tradition.

Beyond contextualization

For many years, missionaries and others have been contextualizing by drawing upon stories, images and practices from the hosting culture. This has been a crucial and important development.

However, contextualization can also result in certain aspects of a culture being clung to, even when it is contrary to how Jesus and the early church embodied power. I experienced this in Africa when a retired missionary suddenly appeared and tried to convince participants in a conference on ordaining women, that women could not exercise power over men for cultural reasons even though in that culture, women leaders had long been doing so. On a TV program in Nigeria, I was asked why churches that had brought them Christianity now were changing their position on LGBTQ+ matters. Contextualization can become an excuse or barrier to change. Too often this is religiously enforced.

Even Christmas has been contextualized. Jesus probably was not born in December, and certainly not in snowy weather. Northern Europeans have contextualized this to fit their climate and seasons. This is quite foreign to areas in the global South where Christianity has spread and grown in recent centuries, yet the carols and traditions have spread there, even though in recent years there has been some contextualizing of hymns and traditions.

Theology has always been contextual. I realized this again while at a Lutheran World Federation (LWF) Council meeting in 2002 in Wittenberg Germany. Those from throughout the world realized how what began there over five hundred years ago arose out of that context in sixteenth-century Germany may seem scandalous to many in the world today (some were scandalized that "they even drank beer which now has Luther labels!"). However, what was imprisoning or locking most people then and there, may not be the lock that is imprisoning people in contexts today.

Contextualization has been pivotal in how it has changed so much of theology. Theologians are realizing that all theology is or should be viewed as contextual. In my first teaching position in the early 1980s, seminary studies began by raising up theology from Black, Latino, feminist and other perspectives—*not* from a normative one-size-fits-all core. This has spread around world, where contextualization has now become what is expected, but usually is not carried out beyond this.

Most of the time, efforts are made to name and analyze a context accurately, drawing from the social sciences and various other disciplines. This is crucial, especially to better understand how a current context may be different from the what presumably was the original context. However, then the explicitly un-examined theological answer tends to be plugged in, in automatic un-examined ways, as if this what is needed or even relevant in the current context. It may not be!

What is locking people down in a current context (such as cultural practices, systemic poverty or repressive government) may be quite different from a context of another time or place. What is liberating news in one context may actually be bad news that reinforces bondage in another. For example, over half a century ago, some of us feminists claimed that the formula "sin as pride" may not be good news to women; this may be changing in some contexts today. What is Good News in a particular context is crucial. I have heard many sermons around the world, where most of the time was focused on unpacking and understanding the present context, with lots of good analytical tools, but after this, the same doctrines were plugged in as answers. Are they really? The usual theological responses also need to be transformed or at least expressed in new ways. Otherwise, theology and churches may increasingly become irrelevant, anemic in speaking to and transforming the real crises at hand.

Jesus transformed power[6]

In my years with the LWF as a communion of churches, power has often been what really is at stake. Churches fear they will lose funding, based on old missionary or colonizing ties; these must be pleased. Power still lies with the big donors.

6. An earlier version of this appeared in an LWF publication.

9

At least it is assumed, how power operates should adhere to practices prevailing in churches of the global North.

Too often these still reflect and reinforce various kind of supremacy over others—including how a male-imagined god is used to justify such, and theological expressions that embody what are foreign assumptions. Hierarchical ways of exercising power and administration still prevail; these become the fall-back. This often is reinforced by long-held cultural patterns. Gospel may be preached and taught, but how power is exercised in church and society is left untouched. Leaders fear and are silent in challenging such.

This is especially in settings where oligarchs actually rule, where those with enormous wealth and power reign, not only in countries like Russia and the United States, but in many other places around the world. Some have become very wealthy due to how they benefit especially from global neo-liberalism.

Being church in much different contexts around the world at times remains an idealistic platitude, or is really tested or contested when certain matters arise—most frequently those related to gender or sexuality. *Culture* becomes the excuse; this triumphs over theology. Overlooked are indigenous practices that may have prevailed long before missionaries came.

Churches that identity themselves as *evangelical* may think they avoid the abuses of power that plague some churches. However, this can result in the concentration of power in the hands of highly charismatic men. Some of these macho celebrities inflict their power on the vulnerable, and especially on girls and women.

As recorded in the New Testament, Jesus was continually crossing boundaries across cultural and religious differences. He dared to cross boundaries between men and women, with those who were considered *foreign*, with those considered *unclean* due to disease or cultural mores, with those who were cast aside as demonic or *evil*. He associated with prostitutes, tax collectors and others assumed to be *sinners*. Expelling sin and evil has often been seen as the church's mission, but through Jesus, we see that sin lies in the very act of expelling. In Luke (6:46), where much of how this new kind of power operates is spelled out, Jesus provocatively asks, "why do you call me 'Lord,' and do not do what I tell you?"

Jesus associated with those ignored or thought of as not important, rather than with the rich and powerful, and how they tend to exercise power. Although many have lived out a nonviolent power of resistance throughout the centuries (they are often thought of as *saints*), this has often been considered unrealistic in how power operates in the real world. This been reinforced by two-kingdoms understandings, that insist how power in the secular realm operates differs from how it operates in the spiritual realm. This overlooks that in many cultures, the spiritual and secular cannot be separated in this way.

There may be no straight line from how Jesus exhibited power. He often did so indirectly through parables and how he related to people around him then. There is no "Jesus manual" for power, which is why leadership and power models are often borrowed from other sources today. But they often miss the mark of how Jesus actually exhibited power.

The *kingdom* Jesus regularly proclaimed was an upside-down understanding of how power tends to operate, including since then in churches. As Jesus provocatively asks , "why do you break the commandment of God for the sake of your tradition?"(Mark 15:3). Power is revolutionary, as Mary's song in Luke 1:46ff predicted. Usual understandings of power and leadership were turned over. Jesus refused to succumb to the devil's temptation to have power (Luke 4:6). He was continually transforming how power is understood and operates, by who Jesus associated with and what he said. He was often confusing his followers when they thought of him as a predictable, powerful religious leader.

The power that flows from Jesus is dedicated to and will bring about a very different world. It is a power *with* others, rather than *over* others. Modeling this kind of leadership and power can bear witness not only in the church but also in the wider society.

Theologizing critiques unjust power, especially dominating power over others, with a much different vision, and with a much different sense of power. It enacts another worldview that is inclusive of those who have been considered *other,* challenging the power over others that currently is reigning and dominating. It does this not in a stand-apart, static way that is imposed from above, but in ways that are collaborative with what actually is occurring here and now. This is *theologizing t*hat can transform power.

Addressing today's crises theologically

Worldliness is what the Radicalizing Reformation movement, provoked by the Bible and today's crises, insisted on in its events and various publications, and in which I participated. As the preface to the 94 theses puts it:

> The rampant destruction of human and non-human life in a world ruled by the totalitarian dictatorship of money and greed . . . requires a

radical re-orientation towards the biblical message, which also marked the beginning of the Reformation. The dominant economic system and its imperial structures and policies have put the earth, human communities, and the future of our children up for sale.[7]

The first section of this Declaration points out that Martin Luther sharply criticized the evolving unjust and oppressive capitalist system. The hegemonic capitalistic model increasingly develops a totalitarian regime with its consequences. Thus:

We confess being part of a "Babylonian captivity" that obstructs both the revolutionary spirit of the Reformation and also people's and civil rights.

We reject all forms of systems and practices that deny freedom, democracy, and peoples' participation.

We call upon people and communities of faith to reject the wisdom of greedy money and to embrace the wisdom of the cross, and to work for reconstructing the economic, political and social systems and religious institutions to ensure the dignity and worth of all humans.[8]

So what does provoke in us today? We live in chaotic times when one presuming to rule over all declares and acts as if he (usually male) alone is god. Whatever *I* say is true, despite what the evidence or facts might indicate. As many such autocrats proclaim: "follow me and what I promise," no matter what the results (or lack thereof); *I* alone will assure success, and you can too. *I* will conquer

---

7. Bloomquist, et al., *Radicalizing Reformation*, vol. 6, 19.

8. https://www.reformation-radical.com/en/wittenberg-declaration

the forces of evil, will make you feel secure. *I* will keep you safe—believe *me*.

In other words, we are confronted not with politicians but with those who act as if they are gods, arbitrary gods, with autocratic if not fascist tendencies. Politics as normal no longer governs, nor do the usual ways the religious and political realms have interacted. Some claim to not being politicians. Crowds gather at emotionally-driven rallies that are much like religious rallies, with words added to give legitimacy to so-called *Christian* battles against the forces of evil. This has also been done tragically by religious figures in the past, such as Martin Luther against the Jews, and whose legacy must be critiqued in this regard. Playing to people's emotions is not new but unfortunately has become common in the arsenal of some leaders. Emotions rule over any rational arguments. Mass emotions are stirred up, but little is offered for effectively governing with policies to make people's lives better.

As Martin Luther put it, a god is anyone or thing is which people place their trust, on which people's hearts rely. Many have been enticed to follow these false gods of our day—for whom acquiring as much wealth and celebrity status as possible is all that matters, Little attention is given to governing that serves the common good, or even what is in followers' self-interest. This is an arbitrary god who regularly changes his mind, surprising us with ever new atrocities clothed as *blessings*, with misleading lies as if they were truths. We are confronted with the absolute idolatry of power of wealth, strength and unaccountable military might. This is what prevails in many countries today.

In contrast, throughout biblical history, the people of God were tempted to and often did follow false gods, which is why cautioning against idolatry is such a major theme throughout the Bible. In much of Scripture, false gods were seen as those worshipped in other religions, but the reigning false gods in our time are those who demonize those of other faiths. Practices based on hardness, toughness and fear are advocated. Certainly there are passages in the Bible that can be selectively drawn upon by hardliners who want to depict this is how God is, but depicted overall is a compassionate God who suffers with the people, redeeming and reconciling, bringing hope not fear.

We must draw on moral principles rooted in our faith for critiquing and resisting various proposals or tweets coming from the reign of any autocrats– especially those based on racist, xenophobic or misogynist assumptions. Resisting and recognizing how different issues intersect with each other is crucial. This has been occurring in many resistance movements today, but may not be sufficient, because the challenges seem so overwhelming and are getting worse. Struggling with others for justice is important, but often this does not go far enough. This is because something deeper is at stake: the whole set of systemic assumptions or worldview. This is what theologizing claims to provide as a counter-view to what is operating. So why haven't people of faith woken up to the need to challenge publicly what is occurring from out of the heart of the faith we confess?

In addition to recognizable practices, such as proclaiming the Word and celebrating the sacraments, this means going beyond the usual Christian boundaries, where Luther tended to stop. This also evokes expressions that are more porous and publicly accessible to others, including those who have minimal religious connections. This involves crossing some of the usual boundaries between sacred and secular, the binary of *us* versus *them*, between local and global realities, between Christians and those of other faiths, between racial/ethnic or other affinity groups, between humans and the rest of nature, in ways that are trans-contextual, transfigurational and thus transformative for the sake of the common good in a world that God creates, loves, redeems and continually transforms.

CHAPTER 2

Aspects of a personal journey

Drawn to California after college

GROWING UP IN WISCONSIN in the 1950s I did not realize how separations and resentments were festering then in what had been a somewhat progressive area (at least some of my teachers) but has now become quite conservative, even reactionary. Nevertheless, those of us preparing for college, and ruled by meritocracy, did not associate with those heading to fight in Vietnam. We did not see the resentment based on classism that was brewing. Instead, my perspectives on the injustices raging in much of the world were connected with the church and theology from outside of my hometown and church. This theology was liberating! I was drawn to attend a church-related college in another state, not the secular university in my state.

In college when some were protesting the injustices raging in the 1960s, and in which I quietly participated, I was drawn to major in religion as well as sociology. I did not intend to defend religious institutions or theology. I critiqued such, and joined those doing so. The women's movement was arising again, so I was especially drawn to this. Suddenly I switched from wanting to do graduate work in theology to pursing ordination. I was encouraged in this not by religion but sociology professors. One of my sociology professors encouraged me to write a thesis on the self-concept of the role of the defiant woman. I was becoming one!

During my senior year, while writing a thesis on the liberated church movement, I was drawn to California for my research. There I encountered developments that have now spread over much of the country, such as the declining size and influence of churches. Theology being released from institutions was already beginning then. This also was more multifaith and justice-focused. Most of all, I met women who were pioneers in studying theology and as pastors in the Bay Area, especially at schools of the Graduate Theological Union in Berkeley. That is where I wanted to go. Yes, I would be the only woman at the Lutheran seminary, and having to challenge the patriarchy that was raging, but I would have other *sisters*, not to mention the challenges of the Bay Area and the budding of *theologizing* in the face of such. Here I began to realize that theology could not remain a body of abstract doctrines but had to connect with what was going on in the world.

I served as the pastor of a church in East Oakland in the 1970s. I was again drawn back to Oakland many years later in 2015. It had become home to me, but now was much different. Although the Black population has declined a lot, despite the Black Panther and other movements beginning here, the rich diversity has otherwise grown. Immigrants from all over the world come here.

Younger artists and activists prevail. Most are not interested in traditional religious institutions or theology.

After nearly 50 years

She wandered over from Mills College, and began attending the congregation for which I was pastor in East Oakland. Born and raised in Pakistan, her perspectives and experiences were quite different from others in this mostly white working class congregation. After some time, she informed me that she had decided to go to seminary, but realized that it probably would be good to be confirmed first, so I confirmed her.

We remembered the same people, some of whom are still with this much changed congregation, and their various problematic issues. She reminded me of how I had cut through new ground (as the first Lutheran parish pastor in the western US), and I recalled how she had accompanied and encouraged me in that. We recalled the older white man who was always speaking out and challenging racism in Oakland and the church, and whose funeral was my last pastoral act in the congregation. This was a big public event in what usually was a sparse church, which that day was filled with folks this man had interacted with throughout the Bay Area and beyond.

After finishing seminary, she never was ordained, but has been employed by organizations addressing those with disabilities. She also has been very politically active, including spending some risky time in Central America, and writing a play on that era. I have thought often of her through the years, and sensed but did not realize how important I had been for her. Occasionally I meet especially women around the world who have made similar comments to me, as "one of the pioneers," or one of the other expressions I have previously been unaware.

Many in our generation have been pioneers in changes that now are being threatened. How can we as elders address what is occurring, from our accumulated experience and wisdom? How can we do that, not in ways that heightens the polarized walls, but from out of feminist (and related) perspectives that reframe what is occurring, theologizing for the good of all?

Influenced by Dorothee Soelle

She was not why I went to Union Seminary in NYC to pursue my doctorate. I was drawn there because it was at the forefront of Black, feminist and other liberation theologies that were emerging in the 1970s, and has influentially shaped much in American society and politics. Between 1980 and 1982, I became the teaching assistant to Dorothee Soelle, a small, frail yet very influential woman who was invited to teach there, rather than in her home country in Germany. At her funeral, the women bishop preaching alleged that the worst sin of universities there was never offering her a position there.

Dorothee was often challenging established theological positions and establishments, as well as much that was going in the Germany and throughout the world—when the arms race and Vietnam War were raging. Her outspoken protests and activism regarding such were pervasive. She was a strong critic of what the US was doing then, and I have often thought of what she would say about what is now occurring. What she wrote and how she spoke to common folks was convincing, such as redefining sin as *when life freezes over*. She often challenged how Germans had been complicit in the Holocaust, and some of her followers were left-wing Jewish leaders, South American peasants, and lots of secular common folks. She wrote many books. She readily embraced democratic socialism, and had early been associated with *death of God* theologians, even though her being rooted in basic faith understandings was unmistakable. Her later book, on mysticism and resistance,[1] was widely lauded and quoted, as were her many other books, especially for those skeptical of any religion.

Because I lived a long way across New York City, I would sometime stay with her in her apartment at Union, where I became more familiar with her simple way of living, and some of the people she knew. When she was back in Germany, she would sometimes phone me, asking if she should accept this or that speaking invitation. In many ways, I was her assistant in the US, as well as her friend.

One morning in the fall of 1982, while riding the NY subway to Union and while pregnant with Aaron, I had morning sickness, and threw up on other passengers. Thus, I arrived late at a class I was teaching with her. She subsequently wrote one of her many poems, this one on not realizing what I, another woman, was going through (she had birthed four children). After Aaron was born, I asked her to be godmother and preacher at his baptism, which took place at a big conference at the seminary, where people I knew from throughout the country were present.

Some years later, a director of the retreat center in the remote Cascade Mountains of WA (Holden Village) where I often taught, asked me to persuade her to come there. She and her husband did come, and for two weeks we shared a chalet. Many early mornings he would take a hike and

1. Soelle, *The Silent Cry.*

encounter bears, who appeared for *this* German. When we departed from there, while waiting for the two-hour ferrry ride, she stripped off all her clothes, and as was her custom, and plunged into the icy water for a swim.

Some years later she died suddenly, just after speaking on "joy" at a big event in Germany. I flew from Geneva up to Hamburg for her funeral, where the big church and the streets around it were filled with people, in honor of one who had influenced so many throughout the world, including me. I was not as bold as she, but theologizing is what she did.

Trust put to a homeless test

For over two weeks in the fall of 2019, I traveled by myself to some of my favorite parts of Italy (Cinque Terra, Tuscany, and Sicily). I had rented a car (in Tuscany and Sicily) and reserved B&Bs in towns I wanted to stay in. Although I spoke no Italian, and did not have a cell phone that worked there, and at this time of the year there were few tourists where I went and it rained at lot, for the most part I eventually found where I wanted to go, guided by an offline GPS, which took me down many narrow roads. I also stopped many people to get directions.

This radical trust—which is at the core of theologizing—was put to the test. In Pisa, I stopped to visit touristy sites (the Leaning Tower and Cathedral), although I parked in a residential area and locked everything, my computer and suitcase (and all my possessions in it) were stolen. So for the rest of my time (about a week) I flew to and traveled through Sicily wearing mostly the same clothes, and carrying only a backpack and plastic bag. But I got by. For the most part I enjoying interacting with the local folks and soaking in the sights of the towns and countryside.

However, then I returned to the US, and starkly experienced the plight of what it is to be without shelter. My solidarity with those long been homeless was not only rhetoric (as it is in much theology) but was put to a personal test. Although I had researched beforehand how to get from Dulles Airport (where I landed) to BWI (Baltimore) from which I was to fly out the next day (after staying at a hotel near the airport where I had reservations), I didn't realize how difficult this would be at night.

After waiting nearly an hour, I took the bus into the Metro DC area. Having done this before I felt good, assisting a young German woman who had just arrived in what she said she experienced as the inhospitable US. By the time I reached the end of the orange metro line (North Carrolton), there were few people left, and the MARC train to the Baltimore airport was no longer running. Shortly (just before midnight) the metro also stopped running. Although the agent reluctantly told me to walk "this way and turn right," I soon realized that there were no hotels or other places to stay within miles of this stop, and the Baltimore airport was still about twenty-eight miles away. The only cab driver would have charged me a lot to get there, and he seemed drunk and not reliable. I approached two white men, who would not help this older bag lady whose story they would not believe.

I walked the streets for over an hour, in the freezing cold weather. The sweater I had bought in Italy at least kept my head somewhat warm. I was tired and cold and increasingly desperate. I even checked out the parking garages to see if there was any cold cement corner where I could plop down in until morning, but I found none.

After walking around, I realized there were a few federal and high tech office buildings in this area, but they were all locked tight. No one was on the streets at this hour. I found one building where there was a real human being, but this security guard, where he saw me, who looked like a home-less bag lady, only wagged his finger at me and refused to come to the window so I might explain and at least stay in the lobby. I was feeling increasingly desperate, and even eyed the train tracks for where I might collapse, even though the train cars probably were all locked. I eventually reached a street where there were a few businesses, but all were closed, even the twenty-four-hour laundromat.

Suddenly, two young African males appeared; they were jiving with one another. I was reluctant at first, but as they approached, we began talking. I told them my plight and who I was (clergy). One of them offered that I could probably stay where he was staying. By this point, I really was desperate, so I accepted his offer, giving him some money and stopping at an open store to get some-thing to eat. He indicated he had gone through bad times, including times of homelessness, but was currently stay-ing with friends. He took my hand to help me down the step hill through trees and roots. This was a shortcut to what was an apartment complex that looked "decent" or at least warm at this hour. After knocking, we went in. In this sparsely finished small apartment sat about half a dozen men, talking loudly and crudely. One who appar-ently was the renter, indicated that it was OK if I stayed there, so with my meager stuff around me, I sat down on the couch that had holes and was disintegrating, and soon laid down in exhaustion. I went to the bathroom, but first had to move the door which was off its hinges, so that I would have some privacy there. I noticed lots of holes in the walls, and dirt in the tub. It now was 1:30 AM but the TV was still blaring close by.

Falling asleep, I realized after an hour that the TV was finally off, and that four of the guys were asleep on or across chairs. As their guest, I was given the couch. At 6 AM, I got up, and slipped quietly out of there, after four hours of sleep. I had survived, thanks to the help of those who knew the desperation of what it is like to be without shelter, which I too have now experienced, but for only a night. Homelessness was now very personal for me, and more than rhetoric.

Fear can entrap us

The COVID pandemic reached ominous new depths, with repeatedly calls for various ways of protecting ourselves that are important, and how we in community need to protect one another. Where this is consistently occurring even in the poorer parts of the world, the incidence of infection was low.

However, have our fears overtaken us, such that they become like a closed petri dish, feeding on and fueling on another? Fears lead us to accuse or judge others, who are not following certain measures, not doing as much as we, with an attitude of "at least what we are doing is more morally pure than others." Fear of what is unknown or invisible can escalate, without further discussion and weighing of the options. Dictators play on and escalate fears.

The fearful person does not see particular individuals, just hateful shades who arouse disgust and can be blamed. Muslims are disgusting. Immigrants are disgusting. Those of the other political party are disgusting. Fear induces herding behavior. The irrationalities of disgust underlie many social evils.

Fears can be legitimate, especially toward those who are most vulnerable because of their health vulnerability, race, economic situation, or where they live. Fears can massage each other, and dig us deeper into our fears. This may especially be the case for those sheltering alone, without bodily contact with a partner. Embodiment, emphasized especially by God becoming incarnate, is central to Christian faith and practice. Being present only virtually, we are not able to touch others members of the body of Christ, much less taste the wine and bread of the Eucharist.

Fears also can exclude expressions or acts of hope. They readily displace any faith that things could and can be different—that another world or reality is possible. This is what theologizing can open up. The alternative to fear is not a "pie in the sky" perspective. It is not an escapism or optimism that ignores how bad things have become. Instead, by entering more deeply into the suffering, including with those throughout the world who are suffering far more than we, faith emerges. The fear of death itself is no longer what prevails. We can *live* rather than being in bondage to our fears.

CHAPTER 3

What is widening inequalities today?

Inequalities escalated by class and meritocracy

WHY IS THERE SO much homelessness today? Why are those who have long advanced class equality now seen as neglecting those who are as working-class or poorer? The Democratic Party is now controlled by those who have "made it" through advanced education, ever more professional jobs, ever higher incomes, thus pushing those who have "not made it" out of high-priced areas, especially areas where hi-tech and corporate power reign, and systemically exclude those who can no longer afford to live there.

Many of us identify ourselves as *liberals* and have benefited from liberal governance and policies. This can also result in unattended consequences, such as the ever-widening gaps that we can now call *ill-liberalism*. Those who do not abide or live by liberal mandates are excluded. Unless they individually earn over $100,000 a year they cannot afford to live in some areas. The inequalities have grown much worse today. Those who have *made it* look down, or feel sorry for those who have not. Liberalism, which can turn into ill-liberal intolerance, today has become an expression of an enlightened professional class. Their core economic and cultural interests are quite different from those who are working-class or poorer. For example, *affordable* housing has become a myth out of reach for most folks. Attempts to solve housing and other forms of inequality are blocked or frustrated, and they push many Black, Hispanic, Native, and other essential workers to live ever further away from these areas.

Why are those who have moved into these areas, who presumably are the "smartest, best, most innovative creators," been unable to solve these problems—especially in areas that are very *blue* politically? They often seem immobilized, not knowing what to do. Putting more money on the problems will not suffice. Housing has become ever more less affordable. Nor will placing guilt upon those who "have succeeded" help, nor will their philanthropic efforts. These may help in the short-term but do not solve the overall problem. It is built into the operating system of inequality.

Much of inequality today has surged because realities of *class* and how it operates and is expressed Class mostly has been ignored in American society and history. This is more than economic. We are assumed to be a class-less society, where anyone can succeed. People long have come here to escape societies where class binds, but how the dynamics of class persist in often overlooked. The governing myth is that everyone can succeed if only the try hard enough. I admit that this meritocracy worked for me. Coming from a working-class family, not only was I able to go to college, and eventually even earned a PhD but had advantages I would not have had otherwise, such as being white.

Now, areas that have long been associated with greater tolerance, and which is why many of us came here, such as urban areas or on the coasts. These areas *have* tolerated a lot of differences, but now are exhibiting growing intolerance toward those of a different class, such as through the NIMBY (not in my backyard) and other movements that oppose more affordable housing. Many progressives say they are for more government or regulation, or for "housing for all," but not when their own interests as homeowners are threatened. Ignoring dynamics of class, compounded by race, have only widened the gaps.

In the late 1970s, in an era of de-industrializaton and largely from what I heard in working-class congregations, I began to focus on the dynamics of class and wrote a theological dissertation and eventually a book on how working-class were experiencing "the (American) dream" being betrayed.[1] In better understanding the dynamics and realities of those who for many generations have been "working class," some deeply spiritual, theological and political matters are at stake—and need to change, not just through individual opportunities but through systemic changes that are grounded in transformative theologizing. People's lives are under the control of others, whether in the workplace, daily life, or even churches. Dynamics of individualism, victimization and privatization mask the contradictions of the idolatry that tragically hold working people in bondage, and enables "the American dream" to betray them again and again.

It is not surprising that those who have long experienced this find the slogan "make America great" so

1. Bloomquist, *The Dream Betrayed.*

appealing some decades later. Ill-liberalism and populism have attractive allures in ways they did not have fifty years ago; they are surging today around the world. What has been exposed now is how working folks are controlled not only by forces of de-industrialization, but also by corporate greed, dis-functional politics, and related ideologies reigning throughout society, including in religious institutions. Powers controlling them have mounted. All is sacrificed for the sake of profit or progress or growth. Politicians have become ever-more captive to economic interests and their own electability. The "winners" of this creed and cult, those who "have made it," now define and shape all of reality. This is epitomized in the triumph of liberalism, which gives allegiance to the equality of all and to meritocracy, but does not deliver for most folks in how it did in the mid-20th century. Many still are attracted to this, but find they cannot afford to live by its false promises.

The *winners*, who have become upwardly mobile through government programs, education and high-earning jobs, are sharply set apart from the *losers*. Enrollment in higher education has dropped precipitously, especially for males of color. The disillusionment with what higher education can bring is setting in, as it was not fifty years ago, when it was take for granted as the route to upward mobility. "Why go to college?" is increasingly being asked now.

The inequalities of income and wealth have gotten a lot worse. These are often economic, but they are also of different cultures and where you reside. There is a huge gap between those who live on the West coast or in the Northeast and the vast "fly over" parts of the country that are usually overlooked but that *do* matter. They are *assumed* to be rural, small town conservatives, racists, and so forth.

These are areas to escape from in order to *make it* on one of the coasts, although many of such areas are where local democracy is thriving. Meritocracy has worked for many.

Those who have been left out are advised to get more education or training so that they too can succeed, but increasingly many are skeptical of this as the solution. The gap continues to grow. The air is filled with conspiracy and inflammatory rhetoric unheard before. Polarization has surged, and many are flocking to candidates who promise nostalgically to return to how life had been.

Some of those left out have protested the systemic control, exploitation, and misunderstandings they have experienced, in their jobs, politics, and other institutions. They are angry. These protests are often written off as racist, right-wing, or populist, but are they really?

Populism in the 1890s was originally quite different from what it is associated with today. Some populists then favored government help, opposed racism, and advocated all kind of toleration. All of this was opposed by the elites and experts and professionals and big money that was controlling the political parties then, and even now. Classism was more apparent then.

However, later populism became associated with anti-intellectualism, and in our day, intellectuals ask, why are some so dumb or/blind as to vote against what is not in their self-interest? This is the opposite of the elitism nurtured through meritocracy. Common folks generally are considered too ignorant or stupid to rule themselves, or to vote for what will benefit them. Subsequently, the mass enlightenment and learning that populists originally favored was passed over to experts with professional degrees and administrative or bureaucratic posts. Whereas once liberalism was democratic, liberals now are highly educated and generally have become quite well-off. For example, this has been the case for many churches that were originally working-class, but whose members now are highly educated. Church-related colleges have promoted and furthered this. No wonder this is protested today by those who have been left out. Liberal politics has failed to deliver.

This is, at least one of the reasons, that many are intrigued by and support the cult of some candidates. How empty or contradictory are the promises is not the focus here. Instead the focus is on how the dynamics of class, which endure for generations, have been ignored by those who *have made it* through their education and meritocracy, and left others behind, and are shaping the injustices that are cutting across much of the world today. This has resulted in even more concentrated corporate power over folks. This is resented.

This also is why there is so much inequality and why living has become so un-affordable in many parts of the country. What is to be done about this? Denouncing the classism gaps, or moving to where these gaps are less will not suffice. Changing the worldview and narrative, and systemic change are necessary. Those who have succeeded do not want to give up their privileges, including where they live. In liberal fashion, they may deplore the gaps and the many homeless around them, but that is where this stops. The growing movements of those who refuse to accept being left out or behind continue to grow in their political strength and influence. They also may be why some become even more susceptible to extremist, racist and anti-immigrant appeals.

Genuine listening to the complaints across class boundaries is necessary and seeking to forge some common ground may help. However, it is also necessary to counter the concentration of wealth, and change the over-all narrative. Lamenting about this gap is not enough. It is not inevitable. Here too transformative theologizing may help close the gap.

Neo-liberalism gone mad

As unique as is this time, today's overall reality has not come out of nowhere. Underlying these outbursts is an ideological ordering that is pernicious, in how it permeates our society and world today. This is rooted in *neo-liberalism*.

Neo-liberalism has come to mean untrammeled ruling-class power, and a vicious assault of the rich against the poor. This is achieved through market mechanisms, fiscal austerity and the penetration of capitalist relations into every possible facet of human life. The result is that all relations become essentially competitive, and other people as rivals for scarce goods. *Everything* is turned into a market transaction, a form of buying and selling. Because this permeates all arenas of life, this becomes a theologizing challenge. People become not citizens, but consumers and human capital. The earth is exploited for the sake of economic profit. The aim is to get rid of any regulations or institutions that get in the way of the flow of neo-liberalism. Systemic cruelty and moral irresponsibility are at its heart.

Under the reigning influence of neo-liberalism, politics has become another kind of market transaction. To succeed in politics one simply needs to master "the art of the deal." This kind of deal-maker or transaction logic or bargaining with God has been countered by faith traditions. For example, at the heart of the Reformation that Martin Luther initiated in 1517 was justification by grace through faith, which countered any kind of works righteousness, or trying to make a deal with God, as well as all the ways people's fears can be manipulated, whether by the buying of indulgences then, or by other false promises that are holding us captive today.

Making a deal, or attempting to win at the expense of those who are vulnerable breeds distrust, lack of compassion and disconnectedness, especially from those who are different from *me* and *my* desire to win. Winning is everything. Endless competition against others is the governing mantra under neo-liberalism, which now reigns over all of life, and is destroying political life as we have known it.

Democracy is reduced to its most transactional structure. Neo-liberalism achieves a feat that the great revolutionary and reactionary movements of the nineteenth and twentieth century never achieved. It is based not on a claim to democratic legitimacy but on a kind of naturalism in which there is no alternative. This maintains its citizens and workforce in a state of insecurity and anxiety. Anyone who takes seriously the threat of the newly empowered reactionary Right and for many on the Left, must take seriously the role neo-liberalism has played in laying out the red carpet for this.

CHAPTER 4

Challenging how popular rhetoric is used

Evangelical

THE WORD *EVANGELICAL* IS repeatedly attached to and distorts what is at the core of Christianity. It is being used instead as a political weapon that polarizes. Tragically, it has done this throughout history. The heart of the Christian message is the gospel that liberates from bondage not only persons but also systems that discriminate. The political agenda of so-called *evangelical* Christianity often is used to excuse or reinforce this bondage, resulting in various forms of bigotry. When this occurs what is Christian is being prostrated: it is reinforcing patterns of sexism, racism, and othering that are contrary to the core of the Gospels, as known through what Jesus said and what he did, especially in how he related to those who were being marginalized.

Throughout the centuries, *evangelical* has been quite contextual, and has varied greatly throughout history.

When the Evangelical Lutheran Church in America was formed in 1987, many wondered what this meant, assuming it was quite right-wing. I was contacted by media folks who assumed the ELCA must have very conservative social positions. At the turn of the twentieth century in America, many whom could hardly been thought of as evangelical today (such as Unitarian/Universalists) were often labeled with this word.

At the time of the sixteenth century Protestant Reformation, those distinguished from Catholics were identified as *evangelical*, which continues throughout many places in the world today. In some places, Protestants still are distinguished from Catholics by this word. Yet in recent years this is disputed, especially since the 1999 signing of the Joint Declaration on the Doctrine of Justification between Lutheran and Catholic churches.

Being *born anew* is hardly what makes one evangelical today. Being born anew with the revolutionary, self- and world-changing power of belief cannot be limited. God is turning the world around. What is key is challenging and changing *systems* of discrimination, not only personal attitudes. Instead, *evangelical*—which often claims to be "spiritual but not political"—has become what is supportive of bigoted political agendas that are in opposition to those who are white, heterosexual, well-off and usually male. This betrays what we read in the Gospels of how Jesus actually related to those who were different sexually, racially, status-wise or by other forms of otherness. He was continually crossing boundaries of what was appropriate—and therein is the Good News for all today.

Abandoning the designation *evangelical* may not be possible today—it is too widely and popularly used. But those who see it at the heart of what gospel means, which must be lived out because of what Jesus said and did, can provide a counter-witness to what the word means. It is the Good News of not fearing the future but embracing those who are different, of crossing boundaries and liberating from bondage. Many are yearning to hear and experience this bold Good News.

Only *Jesus*

How many songs are sung and sermons preached in which repeating the word *Jesus* is always the answer? This often is devoid of any biblical meaning. *Jesus* become an incantation, used to justify almost anything. When the ELCA was beginning, an esteemed professor said to me, liberate us from focusing only on Jesus. As a biblical scholar he knew quite well that Jesus freed many who were in bondage to culture, tradition, and other boundaries and forces. However, this obsession with Jesus as the only one, ignores how Jesus is one aspect of the Trinity, and tends to distance us from interfaith relations. Many are mystified by a Triune God. Yet the relationality and interconnectedness of the Trinity is central to who God is.

Yes, Jesus makes Christianity unique or distinctive. Yes, we worship Jesus because what he said and did reveals God for us. Yes, as Christians, we claim to be united in Christ and all our differences are overcome. However, through the centuries *Jesus* has been misused to exploit or colonize others. In this sense, this may need to be purged if there is to be genuine relating with those who of a different or of no faith. Or can this become re-envisioned in ways that cross all kind of boundaries, including of another faith or even other politics? Is this not what Jesus was about?

Nationalism

The word *Christian* is often attached to the word *nationalism* but this blurs the distinction between Christian identity and national identity. This often supports assumptions about nativism, white supremacy, authoritarianism, patriarchy, and militarism. Under nationalism, those who traditionally are seen as outside a certain ethnicity or religion are ostracized or at least treated as other. Nationalism for many centuries, and even in many places today, justifies any supremacy over others, especially based on nation, ethnicity or religion. Others do not belong here.

For many years, some of us have challenged any expressions of supremacy, or rule over others. *Any* religion can be accused of this—be they Hindi, Sikh, Buddhist, Jewish or Christian. Extremism of any kind is often justified on religious grounds. This is a misuse or manipulation of any religion. It can lead to insults toward adherents of any religion. For example, *all* Christians are written off as of being nationalist extremists. This is anti-Christian discrimination, which may be increasing in some settings.

There is a tragic historical record of how nationalism operates in supremacist ways. Opposing any supremacy is crucial. Assuming that all Christians are nationalists is a slur that ignores that many are challenging how any religion can be manipulated wrongly to support any nationalism or supremacy. Nationalism should not be associated with any religion, but in any religion can be misused, especially when it is used to exclude others.

Religiously-based nationalism of any kind is heresy. This tends to pit some against others, according to binary tendencies. These are culturally foreign to many, even though they may have been inherited through colonizing influences. An example of this is currently occurring in

India under President Modi, in which those who are not Hindu, most notably Muslims, are considered *enemies* of the State. I recall sitting in a church in India there when many rejoiced at the slaughter of Muslims in Pakistan, which for many years was considered the enemy of India. Unfortunately, religion has been used to justify much violence throughout the world.

Rather than conflating religion with nation, dualisms based on binaries must be purged. This pits some against those perceived as enemies. Identities and patriotism become absolutes, over which even wars are fought. This fuels much polarization. This is not new but is expedited today. Much theology through the years has also contributed to this. This includes separating spirit from matter, which has resulted in the denigrating of nature, which climate scientists, and mystics throughout the ages have reminded us. Binary thinking and action often kills us and others. More nuanced thinking and actions are needed.

CHAPTER 5

Moving beyond binaries that polarize

Beyond binaries

BINARY WAYS OF THINKING, in which sides must be taken, contribute to polarization that separates those who are seen as other. Polarization now is persuasive throughout the world, and threatens democracies. Which political party and its positions you identify with or belong to, are in opposition to those who are seen as *other*. The other side is hated, even deemed to be evil. Identities are rooted in binaries—you either are this or that, even though for many their identities are multiple, or inter-sectional. This is epitomized in the binary of either supporting Israel or Palestine. You cannot be for both.

Polarization is not new. In the US, this often was bridged in the mid-twentieth century, but it has intensified since the 1970s. Now it has become toxic. It often is rooted in binaries that are threatening democratic governance today. Many today are moving beyond binaries in how they identify themselves. Those whose identity is neither male not female have led the way: they are both male and female, or transgender. Those who refuse to take sides according to binaries may be leading the way into the future. This is consistent with what Jesus repeatedly said, although there probably is no biblical evidence that he addressed gender identity *per se*.

Yet faith perspectives, from many traditions around the world, and in Jesus, go beyond binary thinking. Jesus came to abolish those very divisions that set some against others. As recorded in the New Testament, Jesus was continually crossing boundaries across cultural and religious differences. He dared to cross boundaries between men and women, with those who were considered foreign, with those considered unclean due to disease or cultural mores, with those who were cast aside as demonic or evil. He associated with prostitutes, tax collectors and others assumed to be *sinners*.

Expelling sin and evil has often been seen as the church's mission, but through Jesus, we see that sin lies in the very act of expelling. In Luke (6:46) where much of how this new kind of power operates is spelled out, Jesus provocatively asks, "why do you call me 'Lord,' and do not do what I tell you?"

Jesus associated with those ignored or thought of as not important, rather than with the rich and powerful, and how they tend to exercise power over others. Although many have lived out a nonviolent power of resistance throughout the centuries (they often are considered saints), this often has been considered unrealistic in how power operates in the real world. This been reinforced by some two-kingdoms understandings, that insist how power in the secular realm operates differs from how it operates in the spiritual realm. This overlooks that in many cultures, the spiritual and secular cannot be separated in this way.

Ethics are rarely either/or, which is what binaries encourage. Be either for Israelis or for Palestinians. You must choose according to binary thinking. You must be either Republican or Democrat. You cannot be for both. People and countries become locked by such binaries. Finding any common ground or values is ruled out. This is not to deny that sometimes a stance against injustices is called for, but even then, it is not self-interests but morality and the interests of others, that prevail, rather than a *me verses others* logic that is rooted in binaries.

Beyond the *pro-life/pro-choice* binary on abortion

There has been a groundswell of appropriate mourning at the ending of Roe v Wade after fifty years. We are entering a new frightening era, especially for women. The polarities of choosing being *pro-life* or *pro- choice* are raging, but they only heighten the divide in the US. Another way must be pursued if we are to emerge out of this quagmire. How might theologizing help to reframe this?

The binary on abortion is that you are either *pro-life* or *pro-choice*. This is an example that keeps us divided. We must move beyond the usual poles and forge some common ground. This is what the ELCA (Evangelical Lutheran Church in America) did in its social statement adopted in 1991, for which I was staff director (and wrote much of this). There were vigorous arguments which included those with quite different perspectives and lived experiences on this, and who eventually did some bridging. The final statement says that "a developing life in the womb does not have an absolute right to be born, nor does a pregnant woman have an absolute right to terminate a pregnancy. The concern for both the life of the woman and the developing life in her womb expresses a common concern for life. This requires that we move beyond the usual 'pro-life' versus 'pro-choice' language in discussing abortion."[1] Although guidance is provided, recognized is that "conscientious decisions need to be made in relation to difficult situation that vary greatly." In public policy it says that "what is moral should not necessarily be enacted into law." This is what the majority in the US now support.

Many on the *pro-life* side insist that life begins with fertilization, but it does not necessarily. For many years, embryology has informed us that most zygotes at that stage then fail to implant, and that not until at least the eighth week after implantation does an embryo become a fetus. These facts change even many who believe that human life begins at conception. A human being is created gradually through complex genetic, physiological, and relational developments. This scientific data was key for arriving at consensus by the task force that developed this social statement.

The narrative based on *pro-life* or *pro-choice* needs to be re-framed if there is to be movement beyond Roe v Wade. Both sides are for life. This is an example of where binary thinking is insufficient. Policies need to be developed that respect values on both sides. Narratives must move beyond *pro-life* versus *pro-choice*. This is non-binary.

1. ELCA, *Abortion* (1991), 2.

New manifestations of empire are emerging

The binary of empire is reflected in the many billions of dollars that the US provides Israel in military aid, even when this is tied to ending human rights abuse of the Palestinians, much less any two-state solution. Any protest of or even reduction in this aid is vehemently resisted. Continual refrains are to keep Israel secure at any cost or "Israel is our ally." Organized lobby work has been carried out to bolster pro-Israel sentiment. Some Israeli security technologies also are used to catch immigrants fleeing across the southern border of the US. Empire operates in interlocking ways.

Perhaps in reaction to this, there has been a dramatic upsurge in incidents of *antisemitism*. These must be decried and opposed, but critiquing what Israel is doing is not. Islamophobia also must be opposed. Silently defending or overtly funding Israel's imperial practices against the Palestinians is not sufficient. Calling for an end to violence is insufficient. This can perpetuate more counter-violence if the causes and reigning narratives are not addressed and changed.

The prophetic goes to the heart of Jewish identity, which is not primarily tied to ethnicity or land. After reviewing a number of notable Jewish writers, Marc Ellis provocatively asked, "Does the Holocaust as central to Jewish identity, and exclusive of others, also force a particular identity upon Jews themselves?"[2] Fixed identities are problematic. The ethical tradition of embracing and living out prophetic critique of injustice is at the heart of Jewish identity. Prophetic critique goes to the heart of what Judaism has long been about.

2. Ellis, *Encountering the Jewish Future*, 180.

Naming what is occurring in Israel as *apartheid*, as most of the world now does, does not take away from the distinctive atrocities of the Holocaust. This acknowledges that apartheid practices in South Africa—not unique there—now apply to practices that occur under empire configurations elsewhere, particularly in how Israel treats Palestinians.

Guilt over what happened in the Holocaust cannot hold back churches and others, as often happens in the US and Germany. Ongoing guilt, as religious traditions have long advocated, is not the stopping point. As Psalm 102 puts it in verse 12, "as far as the east is from the west, so far [God] removes our [guilt] from us." As thesis #14 of Radicalizing Reformation says: "Luther returns to the biblical truth that God forgives with no exceptions, and out of this forgiveness grows the trust that grounds solidarity with the neighbor."[3] Thus, guilt is transformed into prophetic opposition to unjust practices that are now occurring, which also are practices of apartheid that separate people. Peace between Israel and Palestine cannot occur without righting systemic injustices.

The war in Ukraine, which has resulted in horrendous destruction, has exposed and drawn the world back to the old binary narrative of the Cold War era: "the East versus the West." Thousands are dying. Throughout the world, many are questioning this narrative. The Ukrainian conflict has exposed how empire operates today, such as through standoffs between empires of the East (especially of Putin's Russia) and the West (the US and NATO). Countries that may want to negotiate a peace between Russia and the West are suspected because they are not with one side or the other. They are refusing to being drawn into

3. Bloomquist, *Radicalizing Reformation*, 23.

this conflict and are accused of having self-interests at stake. Self-interest may play a role, but something else is also going on. Leaders of Iran have come to Nicaragua to discern how the influence of the US can be countered. The president of Brazil has taken a Ukrainian peace proposal to China, and together they have agreed to counter the dominance of "the West." However, "the West verses the East" still is the framing narrative. Neutrality is ruled out. So too are initiatives to negotiate peace.

Countries in the global South too often have been overlooked, even though eight of the nine billion in the world today live there. In many of these countries, practices of empire, especially through many decades of the reign of neo-liberalism, have been long protested. Their perspectives are changing the narrative of how the US driven empire operates, including through NATO. Even long-neutral Finland and Sweden now are joining and taking sides. The West writes off refusing to take sides: how could China, India, Brazil or South Africa help, other than by providing arms? What if Saudi Arabia and Iran ally together, and what might this mean for Israel?

New configurations of empire, and resistance to such, are emerging. Many are now challenging how the US monopoly of empire has operated; this now may be changing. Empire sometimes operates in blatant ways, as in Putin's Russia, and must be resisted. But much harder to resist is how empire operates more indirectly through other countries or coalitions or corporate practices, as the US and others do, not only with regard to Israel and the Ukraine, but also in many other ways throughout the world. This is what *theologizing* for the sake all exposes and the operating binary narratives that need to be transformed.

CHAPTER 6

What is needed?

Practice grass-roots democracy

ALARMING IS THE POLARIZING fear of the other and how
this is attracting authoritarian appeals and leading to the
emerging of fascism around the world. Authoritarian rul-
ers have become *antichrists*. In contrast, all are created in
God's image, which must be respected, and their participation in governance encouraged. At the heart of most faiths
is reconciliation with those often seen as other.

This is not another sobering discussion of how democracy seems to be declining in the US and around the
world. Democracy is! But we must move beyond deploring
this. Democracy is not static and is never fully reached,
even in supposed paragons of this. Nor will theoretical discussions about democracy suffice, which may be quite different depending on the context. Many in other contexts
are suspicious of the very word *democracy*.

Instead, the focus here is on actual *practices* that
together are building up resistance to polarization and

emergent expressions of fascism, which also is ever-changing with different manifestations globally. These practices are often locally-based. They provide grounds for hope, rather that only despair about the decline of democracy. They also are practices of theologizing.

Fascism is used not only to remind us of past incidents of this and the horrible ends to which it led in the past, but also alerting us to how fascism may be emerging in interconnected ways in our time. Fascism stands for a coherent set of ideas that are potentially more dangerous than authoritarianism or an individual tyrant. To fight these overlapping ideas, it is necessary to be aware of what they are and how they fit together. Jason Stanley puts it bluntly: "Fascist leaders are 'men of action' with no use for consultation or deliberation; the value of expertise is rejected; the goal is not to convince but to sway the will."[1]

These interlocking features are present in many contexts around the world today. They re-enforce each other, and often depend on an authoritarian leader, who may even become a cult hero with many followers. They are not seen first as fascist but their policies can lead to this. They pit some against others, thus intensifying polarization.

How can practices of democracy be nurtured that provide a basis for resisting what is occurring? Agreeing to disagree, or attempts to develop values of common ground is not popular, and may need to be taught more today. This talking together across divides is occurring in many local communities. The media tends to focus on examples of where this has broken down, sometimes even leading to violence. Where this quest for common ground is taking place is usually overlooked. Many organizations

---

1. Stanley, *How Fascism Works*, 52, 53.

are seeking to promote this, and are developing guidance for doing so. What follows are only three examples of such practices.

Braver Angels[2] has developed approaches for doing this in families and in communities between those those who lean *red* and those who lean *blue*. They are not afraid of discussing controversial, polarizing issues, even with opposing politicians in Washington, DC. Since its founding in late 2016, Braver Angels has held thousands of workshops, trainings and debates across the American country that bring ordinary citizens together across the political divide, and has measurably reduced polarization. Many of these are locally-based alliances. In 2019, they began adapting and piloting its programs with elected officials, candidates, and political staff at all levels of government. Listening to those on the other side is key.

In a *Civility First* forum I attended in 2023 in WA state, between a Republican state senator and the Democratic lieutenant governor, it was evident how much they had become friends though the practice of finding values they hold in common. The lieutenant governor, who presides over the state senate, observed that there has been more civil discourse there than probably in fifty years. He also leads with others the bipartisan project on Civic Health, one of many such efforts today.

This has also been occurring globally, such as in communities in Africa and Asia. An example are the Interfaith Peacemaker Teams, being organized and trained through *OMNIA* (Institute for Contextual Leadership),[3] which has thousands of trained peacemakers and well over two hundred and fifty teams in Bangladesh, Indonesia, Liberia,

2. www.braverangels.org.
3. www.omnialeadership.org.

Nigeria, Sri Lanka, Togo, and Uganda. These are organized in local communities, especially where those of different faiths work together on practical challenges in their contexts. In many contexts, food security is the issue. Local communities identify what *for them* are the survival matters. They often (65 percent) are led by women, and those from other marginalized groups. In areas where conflict can rage, often fueled by different faith identities, the result is to bring peace through working together.

Working for peace is a goal of most religions and community groups. This cannot remain a theoretical abstraction. Polarization and fascism must be actively resisted. One way is through regular *practices* that are locally rooted and nurtured—in families, local communities, and countries. Through this, trust in democracy, in which *all* participate, eventually can be restored.

Enact a worldview that moves beyond binaries

Over fifty years ago, many of us began to realize that worldviews that led to dominating, conquering, making a profit from other people or parts of the created world would not suffice. Writing about different worldviews, especially of those previously left out (those of another gender, orientation, race/ethnicity, class, more indigenous parts of the world) was occurring then. Many songs then looked toward a new world of justice and peace. Folk songs sung in the 1970s bring back nostalgic memories. New music has continued and expanded significantly, but the overall situations of injustice have gotten even worse, not only in the U.S. but throughout the world. The inequities have become more stark. Although many (usually academics) were writing about different worldviews, many felt left out of these discussions, resulting in today's resentments and *cancel culture* cries. A shortcoming is that these other worldviews were talked about but not enacted.

Global then was a positive trend, but today *globalization* has become suspect. In the late 1960s, when I was in the first global study group at my college (in Ethiopia, India, Thailand and Japan), my eyes were opened to much different worldviews than those to which I was accustomed. This has continued throughout my life, including during my time as a director with the Lutheran World Federation when I become even more aware of how people around the world experienced and saw theological and other realities quite differently. Driven especially by colonialization and capitalism, neo-liberal globalization was experienced and viewed far more negatively than it was then in the US.

What began over fifty years ago, although inspired for years, now calls for passing the baton, so that younger, more people of color and others previously excluded now can lead, and not only talk about but actually *enact* new worldviews. Those who still are activists need to support and stand in solidarity with those who are organizing and active today, which often are with different analyses and actions from those of some decades ago. A new world, with new cultural expressions through music, art, film, poetry, and dance, and new worldviews, is growing. Former institutions and ideologies, are changing; they are dated and may no longer be credible. "The times they are a-changing" was idealistically sung fifty years ago, but there have been many setbacks since then. Where lies hope for change now?

This means not just repeating the same slogans and analyses. They now have become political fighting and fundraising words, and often lead to increasing polarization.

There is a need for new language and strategies that go beyond what has been. *Liberal* or even *progressive* labels are insufficient—they continue according to Western linear logics and worldviews that increasingly are questioned. Can this be re-framed, move beyond *us vs. them* politics, in ways that affirm new-found identities, but in ever-transforming intersectional, fluid and not rigid ways? How can these be connected in new ways and result in actual transformative changes today? A example of this was in a concert by a woman from Japan, and her husband from Colombia, who together combined their distinctive music and instruments for a new sound.

Worldviews are sustained and nourished through spirituality. New worldviews cannot be birthed apart from spirituality. This is often overlooked as societies become increasingly secularized and often agnostic or atheistic. Instead, political or cultural positions become absolute *gods*, such as struggles for social justice, or ends in themselves. No wonder culture wars and polarization have increased.

Spirituality is quite different from religion, especially in its institutionalized forms. Many have left institutionalized religion, such as churches, synagogues, mosques or temples, but they continue to rely on age-old residual spiritualities. Under westernization, this appropriation is usually quite individualistic, not communal, even though it may have been originally, and thus are adopted in ways consistent with the reign of individualism. Pick and choose for yourself is practiced.

Many spiritual traditions have embraced nature, or have sought to heal the split between humans and the rest of nature. They have adopted past traditions that were branded as pagan or heretical. The age-old rift with nature eis being overcome in many rituals, liturgies and practices, including in churches. Re-emerging are creation-centered theologies and practices that are embedded in various spiritual traditions that have been overlooked. Worldviews that seem to be new but are actually quite old are increasingly popular. But there are deep spiritualities behind these worldviews. Re-imagining is what spiritual traditions have emphasized.

Rather than only changing policies and practices according to prevailing ideologies, by making small changes in policies related to racism, health care, policing, and climate change, what is needed now are changes into overall, more integrated worldviews. This is a distinctive *theologizing* endeavor. It focuses on holistic, underlying reality, and is transformative of overall systems. This goes beyond being *liberal* or *conservative.* It is interfaith—drawing upon age-old traditions and worldviews that may not be considered *religious* and that attract those with no particular religious faith. Advocacy of different policies for the sake of what furthers the good of all is important, but this needs to be re-framed and connected with or articulated from out of an overall worldview, and not primarily driven by ideological commitments, especially those that set some against others (such as Democrats and Republicans), and often lead to alignments and blockages in which no actual change occurs. Profiting or raising funds from these polarizing tendencies loom large. Countless emails plead us to donate to defeat the other side.

Too often humans and the rest of nature are set over and against each other, especially for the sake of what is profitable for humans, but often to the detriment of the rest of nature. We are realizing this through climate change. A different worldview can overcome separations. We are inter-connected with the rest of nature. For example, *rights of nature* are emphasized in the tribal court case of the White Earth Band of the Ojibwe. What is not human has its own intelligence, a different worldview. My dog often *tells* me this. We are interconnected together, even with what may seem strange, even foreign. Hierarchical control or supremacy over nature itself needs to be overcome. Many writers and movements have advocated such.

This goes against what has characterized Western logic, which is naming everything so that they can be distinguished. Putting all in separate categories, so as to distinguish and rule over them, whether plants, animals or human beings, becomes important. Everything needs to be named or categorized. This is a result of this logic. It is what occurs when human beings are sorted by presumably racial differences, and is at the core of what justifies racism and all kinds of other supremacy, including how nature is used. Categorizing legitimates supremacies. It forms a *rational* basis for dominating others, especially when fueled by power.

Culture and spirituality are intertwined for the majority of peoples around the world. They simply cannot be addressed separately, because spirituality includes economics, politics, and so forth. It is part of the whole. The shortfall, especially of Western developed societies, is in not realizing this. Being human cannot occur from some kind of faith or spirituality. I saw a Snohomish banner that proclaims, "Before we were human, we existed in a spiritual world." Spirituality shapes worldviews; they are deeply interconnected. Being in community with others is how faith is expressed throughout the world.

In our time, this increasingly is occurring, especially in the West, by encountering and embracing spiritualities that are not Christian-based. Fears of syncretism with other traditions is fading, even though some resist such, and want to return to the supposed purity of how things have been. An example is organized resistance in some communities to practices of mindfulness, without acknowledging and affirming its Buddhist origins. Keeping spirituality pure or untainted from that of others is considered essential by those who object.

Yet more is involved than blending spiritualities for the sake of lowest common denominators. Each is concerned with what is good for all, especially for those most vulnerable. Each is connected with an overall worldview, which must be recognized and appreciated on its own terms. This may be expressed through dance, visual art, drama, music, or other practices. Spiritually-based worldviews, but not necessarily religious institutions, are needed. Community is essential, and sustains people in struggles of justice. What is important is not only resisting but also re-imagining power that in ways that go beyond binary worldviews.

Focusing on what will serve the common good of local communities crosses many of the divides today, such as all that now divides Democrats and Republicans in the US. In a virtual town hall, hosted by three legislators in one district, bipartisanship clearly was on display. Not only do they (one Democrat, two Republicans) regularly work together, but each testified how they have co-sponsored legislation with someone from the other party. It perhaps is not surprising that most of the legislation enacted recently in that state, has been initiated in bipartisan ways. This is the case in many local communities and states.

Appreciating the worldviews and stories of others is crucial, for the birthing of new movements together. This involves crossing the usual divides. In this sense, the intersectionality of diverse justice struggles can be promising. With careful listening to others, it can lead to indepth solidarity across forces that divide, and action together to confront injustice and end supremacy of all kinds from out of a different worldview.

Theologizing is an ongoing process

The word *theologizing* is used here because it cannot become fixed or static as theology can. It embraces other worldviews. Theologizing is an ongoing process that is connected with actual practices, and is in dialogue with others. It is not the final word. It does not close off conversation, as theology often does. Although it is rooted in some basic even distinctive tenets, what these mean will vary depend on timely, contextual challenges.

Theologizing is what should occur in every sermon, in a given time and place. If theology is only brought in at the end, it often becomes mostly a platitude. The hard work of theologizing is avoided, in the face of contextual challenges confronting us today. In this sense, theologizing is a step beyond but rooted in contextualization.

Theologizing is closely connecting with practices of *diakonia*—living out the faith that is confessed. *Diakonia* implements what is confessed, not for the sake of God but for neighbors in need. Faith-based organizations have done a lot of this, throughout the world, for many years. The focus is not just on beliefs, but on the practicalities of what is needed now and for the sake of the future for all. It is reflection on practice. It leads us to collaborate with those of other faiths, and with civil society. This can occur as a result of theologizing.

Rather than being captive to untruths, illusions, and false promises that popularly appeal to many, and with policies and practices based on hardness, exclusion and fear, we seek to be faithful to a God of compassion and justice, who brings hope, reconciliation and redemption for all. It is this kind of faith-based vision that contrasts with what currently is reigning, and empowers us to work with others to change unjust realities in this faith *kairos.*

The cues and leadership for this today need to come from those who previously have been left out, with the rest of us joining together in solidarity with them. This necessitates collaborating across generations, drawing on the experience and wisdom of those who are older together with those who are younger, and with those who have been split apart, for the sake of greater justice for all today.

Bibliography

Bloomquist, Karen L. *The Dream Betrayed: Religious Challenge of the Working-Class*. Minneapolis: Fortress, 1990.

Bloomquist, Karen L., Craig L. Nessan, Hans G. Ulrich, eds. *Radicalizing Reformation: North American Perspectives*. Zuerich, CH: LIT, 2016.

—————. ed. *Transformative Theological Perspectives*. Vol. 6. The Lutheran World Federation Series: Theology in the Life of the Church. Minneapolis: Lutheran University Press, 2009.

Ellis, Marc H. *Encountering the Jewish Future*. Minneapolis: Fortress, 2011.

Evangelical Lutheran Church in America. "Social Statement on Abortion, 1991." https://www.elca.org/faith/faith-and-society/social-statements/abortion.

—————. *Evangelical Lutheran Worship*. "Hymn #723." Minneapolis: Fortress, 2006.

Larson, Roy. "Prophet for the 80s Fights Racism." *The Chicago Sun-Times*. April 9, 1983.

Soelle, Dorothee. *The Silent Cry: Mysticism and Resistance*. Translated by Barbara and Martin Rumscheidt. Minneapolis: Fortress, 2001.

Stanley, Jason. *How Fascism Works: The Politics of Us and Them*. New York: Random House, 2020.